CU00695129

NEVER GIVE UP

NEVER GIVE UP

Jack Ma In His Own Words

EDITED BY SUK LEE AND BOB SONG

AN AGATE IMPRINT

CHICAGO

Printed in the United States

Library of Congress Cataloging-in-Publication Data

Names: Lee, Suk (Freelance editor), editor. | Ma, Yun, 1964
- contributor.
Title: Never give up : Jack Ma in his own words / edited by Suk Lee and Bob Song.
Description: Chicago : Agate/B2, [2016] | Series: In their own words
Identifiers: LCCN 2016014825 (print) | LCCN 2016027722 (ebook)
| ISBN 9781572841895 (paperback) | ISBN 1572841893 (paperback) |
ISBN 9781572847798 (ebook) | ISBN 1572847794 (ebook)
Subjects: LCSH: Ma, Yun, 1964---Quotations. | Business--
Quotations, maxims, etc. | BISAC: BUSINESS & ECONOMICS
/ Management. | BUSINESS & ECONOMICS / Leadership. |
BUSINESS & ECONOMICS / Entrepreneurship. | BIOGRAPHY &
AUTOBIOGRAPHY / Business.
Classification: LCC HC426.5.M327 N49 2016 (print) | LCC
HC426.5.M327 (ebook) | DDC 650.092--dc23
LC record available at https://lccn.loc.gov/2016014825

10 9 8 7 6 5   18 19 20 21 22

B2 is an imprint of Agate Publishing. Agate books are available in bulk at discount prices. For more information, go to agatepublishing.com

From Bob Song: To my family, who has been super supportive

From Suk Lee: To all dreamers and entrepreneurs who are not afraid to fail, to give birth to their passion and dreams

TABLE OF CONTENTS

INTRODUCTION

Born September 10, 1964, Jack Ma, or Ma Yun (马云), is a Chinese entrepreneur and philanthropist. He is the founder and executive chairman of the Alibaba Group, one of the world's most successful Internet-based companies. With an estimated net worth of $21.8 billion, Ma is one of the wealthiest individuals on the planet.

His journey to the top is a true rags-to-riches story. Before creating Alibaba, Ma was a humble English teacher at Hangzhou Normal College. During a trip to Seattle, Washington, in 1995, a friend introduced Ma to the Internet. After searching for the words "beer" and "China" and finding no results, Ma decided to start an Internet company and bring the World Wide Web to his country. He knew nothing about coding or computers, and few Chinese people understood what the Internet was, let alone its potential in the marketplace, prompting Ma to call himself "a blind man riding on the back of a blind tiger." Despite these obstacles, Ma was determined to start his business. He borrowed money from relatives and set up an office with 17 partners in his small apartment in Hangzhou. In the beginning the company made no money. It gave its services away for free, expanded too quickly, and came close to folding. After many false starts, Alibaba eventually built a platform for small- and medium-sized Chinese businesses to connect to international buyers, and by its third year, the company was finally profitable. Ma's unique vision, positive spirit, and ceaseless determination have helped Alibaba become the most dominant e-commerce company in China today.

One of Ma's most famous mottos, "Never give up," reflects the attitude with which Ma has faced rejection throughout his life. He flunked his university exams twice, finally accepting a spot at what he calls "my city's worst university." Later on, Harvard's graduate school rejected him 10 times. When Kentucky Fried Chicken came to China, 24 people applied for jobs, and 23 people were accepted—he was the only person denied a position.

In 2015, *Forbes* named him one of the 22 most powerful people in the world. Since Alibaba went public on September 19, 2014, and raised a record-breaking $25 billion IPO, Jack Ma and his company have been hot topics in the media world. He is the first mainland Chinese entrepreneur to appear on the cover of *Forbes* and has been in broadcasted conversation with journalists such as Charlie Rose and leaders such as President Barack Obama.

Known for his humility, colorful candor, and exuberant personality, Jack Ma is a highly respected business icon in China. It's no wonder why: Alibaba has been instrumental in revolutionizing the country's commerce and entrepreneurship. It has established not only a first-class network for local and global business transactions but also a previously unheard-of method for trustworthy online payment (Alipay). Before Alibaba, China was a sea of millions of small- and medium-sized enterprises (SMEs) with no easy way to connect to customers or collect payment. For nearly two decades, Ma and his team have strived to create a positive, lucrative business environment for these operations, and Jack Ma has consistently eschewed and challenged the idea that the desires of Alibaba's shareholders should take precedence over the desires of its customers and employees. Because of Alibaba's focus on empowering SME owners, millions have been able to earn decent livings and support their families, a responsibility Ma never seems to take lightly as he looks ever toward the future and Alibaba's goal of helping "2 billion consumers in the world shop online." Generous with his own employees, Ma is not a typical executive chairman. He has been known to provide all-expenses-paid wedding ceremonies and over-the-top performances, like his costumed rendition of "Can You Feel the Love Tonight" at Alibaba's 10th anniversary celebration.

This book aims to provide readers around the world with a better understanding of Jack Ma through his own words, quoted from news articles, public statements, television interviews, and more. Although Ma speaks fluent English and is often interviewed on US media, we have also spent hundreds of hours mining content from Chinese media outlets, including coverage in China's biggest newspapers and television shows, as well as speeches from Alibaba's regular network operators meetings, which are multicity roadshows that allow Ma and his associates to teach local Alibaba users about services and business best practices. Quotations from these sources have been translated from the original Chinese, making Ma's valuable insights—on entrepreneurship, business values, e-commerce, charity, competition, and more—accessible for the first time to an English-speaking audience.

What emerges is a portrait of a man who has, in less than one generation, revolutionized the Chinese marketplace and the world of e-commerce at large—with absolutely no previous experience with business, technology, or frankly, success. This book is for anyone with a dream and ambition—or anyone who needs a little reminder to "never give up."

—Suk Lee and Bob Song

PERSONAL

••

Technological Ability

I'm not good at technology. I was trained to be a high school teacher. It's a funny thing. I'm running one of the biggest e-commerce companies in China, maybe in the world, but I know nothing about computers. All I know about computers is how to send and receive email and browse.

—Asia Game Changer Awards ceremony, 2014

••

Achieving Balance

I love tai chi. Tai chi is a philosophy. [It's] about yin and yang. Tai chi is about how you balance . . . I use tai chi philosophy in business: calm down, there is always a way out, and keep yourself balanced. Competition is fun. Business is not like a battlefield where you die and I win. In business, even if you die, I may not win.

—interview with Charlie Rose, World Economic Forum, January 23, 2015

••

Learning English

I learned my English by myself when I was 12 years old, for whatever reason, I don't know—I just fell in love with the language. Every morning at five o'clock I rode a bicycle 40 minutes to the Hangzhou Hotel looking for foreign tourists to teach me English. I would show them around the city, and they would teach me English.

—Asia Game Changer Award ceremony, 2014

••

Not Stupid

I'm crazy, not stupid.

—*Jack Ma's Quotations on Entrepreneurship*, 2008

••

Blind Tiger

In the past 15 years that I've been working, I've called myself "a blind man riding on the back of a blind tiger." Those experts riding horses, they all fell. We survived because we worried about the future. We believed in the future. We changed ourselves.

—Asia Game Changer Award ceremony, 2014

BUSINESS PRINCIPLES

· ·

Common Values

A common mission, values, and goals are mandatory in any company or organization. Without these three things, you cannot succeed.

—Ningbo Network Operators Meeting, June 11, 2002

When we employ a person, we choose those who identify with our company values. No matter a person's individual talents, they must identify with our culture and ideals. From the first day of training, we talk about common values and team spirit. Together, this leads ordinary people to extraordinary achievement.

—"Jack Ma's Management," February 25, 2004

••

Company Hierarchy

We adhere always to placing the customer first, employees second, and shareholders third.

—Alibaba's 10th anniversary celebration,
September 10, 2009

••

Building Strong Infrastructure

Our system does not rely on one or two people. If I leave and the company collapses, then it wasn't well constructed.

—APEC 5th e-Business Champions Grand Awards
Ceremony, August 2, 2008

••

On Counterfeiting Allegations

How can you sell Gucci or whatever branded bag for so much money? It is ridiculous. I understand the branded companies are not happy, but I also say that's your business model. You have to check your business model, too.

—*Forbes*, November 4, 2015

Motivation to Sell

A salesperson should not think about money but should consider how their product can help the customer's success and be useful to others. This will help their self-confidence and sales ability.

—Qingdao Network Operators Meeting, July 22, 2005

On Economic Recovery

Two days ago, I had a dinner with my Singapore friends and they said, "Our government is encouraging us to have more babies because people are aging and there aren't enough kids." Every country, every nation, needs an incentive package to have more small- and medium-sized companies, to have more hopes. Every big company comes from a small business. Without this kind of hope, without this incentive to have more "babies," we're going to die. Why do I always feel excited? I have eight babies. In the past 15 years, I have built up eight companies. Seven of them are very healthy, and one of them—I sold it. When I look at my babies, Alibaba, Taobao, Alipay, and all the other companies—Ali-Cloud, we just had a new baby two months ago—I always feel excited because you see the hope, and you know, "This baby is going to change me. This baby is going to change the world."

—APEC SME Global Summit, 2009

· ·

Key Performance Indicators (KPIs)

Same as everybody else, I hate KPI! It causes us to lose sight of our ideals and goals and exhausts us in several ways. It diminishes our working inter-est, innovation, and passion. So, we hate it, but we can't do without it! Really, the problem isn't KPI itself but rather the people who design and imple-ment it.

What is KPI? KPI measures indicators in the re-alization of work targets. Without it, we lack spe-cific indicators for evaluating work performance. It doesn't mean, however, that only through KPI can we complete good work. KPI is like going to the doctor where he takes your temperature, blood pressure, and blood for analysis. While it might prove you're not sick, it doesn't absolutely prove that you're healthy either.

—*Jack Ma's Management Diary*, 2009

· ·

Deception

Never deceive others, in business or in life. In 1995, I was deceived by four companies—four companies that are now closed. A company can-not go far by deceit.

—Shanghai Network Operators Meeting, July 2005

Succession Planning

Almost all of our vice presidents have stayed with us through the years. Still, it is important to have successors ready for staff replacement. The company should not be held hostage by key employees, nor those employees by the company. I myself was kidnapped by Alibaba several years ago. I let four key staff members take their holidays in shifts and study abroad for two to three years—meaning that I couldn't go anywhere.

Some say that Jack Ma "eliminates" his company's senior workers. But our successor system needs to be ready for those who have worked for decades and may be too tired, who have no friends except for their work colleagues. While it may appear that there is never a good time for them to take a leave of absence, they must. Once they are forced to do so, your younger workers will have their opportunity. We believe this in our hearts.

—Beijing Network Operators Meeting,
March 17, 2008

•••

Criticism

Criticism from the media, Internet commentators, and investors isn't our concern, only how users and business people respond. If their response is negative, we will be out of business.

—Digital China Forum, China Beijing International
High-Tech Industries Week, May 11, 2001

•••

Corporate Responsibility in the 21st Century

The world is calling for a new commercial civilization. In the old commercial civilization, enterprises were self-centered and profit-centered instead of being society-centered. In the 21st century, enterprises should reconsider their relationship with society, the environment, humanity, and their clients. Today's enterprises must learn transparency, sharing, responsibility, and globalism to make for a better life in the 21st century.

—Alibaba's 10th anniversary celebration,
September 10, 2009

. . . .

Patience

It takes 30 percent of your time to lay the foundation when building a house. A good company, one with a stable and sizable income, needs at least five years for success. . . . Alibaba has not completed laying our foundation. We run our business not because others are doing it or because others wish us to do so. We do it because we believe in what we do, when we should do it, and how we should achieve it.

—ChinaByte.com, July 2001

. . . .

Perfectionism

Before I first went to Japan, my general impression of Japanese companies and businessmen was positive. Not only did they attach importance to rules and etiquette but they did things diligently, dedicating attention to perfection.

I was surprised, however, once I visited Japan. Big enterprises there often delayed decisions and lost opportunities due to trivial things. While I respect people who seek perfection, it's fatal for an enterprise to delay decisive action when time and circumstance demand speed for success.

—*Nikkei Business,* May 2002

• •

Wild Dogs and White Rabbits

We assess employees on two standards: performance and team spirit. . . . Those with high performance but no team spirit are "wild dogs," and those with a good team spirit but low performance are "white rabbits." No dogs or rabbits as employees, please; they must excel at both.

—Xiamen Network Operators Meeting,
September 2001

• •

On Hiring

Hire the person best suited to the job, not the most talented. This can be a very painful lesson. There's no point putting in a Boeing jet engine when you need to run a tractor.

—Dongguan Network Operators Meeting, March 2005

• •

Investing in Employees

Money is better invested cultivating your company's talent through training and organization than in market promotion. Employees need to understand your company, your clients, and your competition. As the Chinese saying goes, "Know your enemies as you know yourself."

—*Nikkei Business*, May 2002

ALIBABA AND OTHER VENTURES

....

Early Days

First week, we have seven employees. We buy and sell, ourselves. The second week, somebody started to sell on our website. We bought everything they sell. We had two rooms full of things we bought for no use, all garbage, for the first two weeks—in order to tell people that it works.

—Economic Club of New York, June 9, 2015

....

Smiling

Smiling is very important to the culture at Alibaba. Our logo is a smile. When our employees and clients go home, I want them to be smiling. While I can't remember the face of every person who comes by the office, I identify if they are Alibaba staff by their smile.

—speech to Alibaba executives, June 16, 2006

∙∙

Business Model

We are not an e-commerce company, although we have the largest e-commerce business in the world. We're not eBay. We do not buy and sell. We help people become an e-commerce company. We enable other companies to do e-commerce. This is the difference between us and Amazon. We believe every company should be an Amazon. Amazon is a traditional business that happens to have a website.

—interview with Jerry Yang, Stanford Graduate School of Business, September 24, 2015

∙∙

Not Simply a Chinese Company

Our dream was to create the best company in the world. Although Alibaba was started by a Chinese person, we aspire to be a global company of investors, employees, and clients, not simply a Chinese company. Decisions are driven by asking how do we become better, not based on the value of our shares. Jack Ma wishes to prove that an Internet company's value comes from wisdom, strategy, courage, and teamwork, not capital.

—*Fortune Life Program*, March 29, 2003

. . . .

Thinking Differently

Our employees are trained to think the Alibaba way.
No matter where they work in the world, they must
come to Hangzhou for a month to learn both our
mission and value concepts and company culture.
Without this, they can't become Alibaba employees.
We spend two hours telling trainees that their ac-
tions reflect their thoughts. Most of the time, sales-
men think of how to get ¥5 from your pocket into
theirs. Alibaba employees need to consider how
they can keep that ¥5 in your pocket and change it
into ¥50. Thinking this way makes us different.

—Dongguan Network Operators Meeting,
March 2005

. . . .

Focus

Our concentration on e-commerce is persistent.
Ten years ago, we concentrated on e-commerce,
and we still concentrate on e-commerce. Ten years
ago, we focused on medium and small companies,
and we will still concentrate on medium and small
companies. Because we concentrate on e-commerce and small and medium companies, we will
operate for a long time.

—Alibaba's 10th anniversary celebration,
September 10, 2009

· ·

Women in Business

One of the secret sauces of Alibaba's success is that we have a lot of women . . . 47 percent of the employees of our company are women. We actually had 51 [percent], but we acquired some companies and they had more men, so the balance [went] down. Thirty-three percent of the management are women, and 24 percent of the senior management—very top level—are women. We have a woman CEO, CFO, CPO. . . . If you want to win in the 21st century, you have to make sure you are making other people powerful. Empower others. Make sure the other people are better than you are, and you will be successful. So I find that women think about the others more than they think about themselves.

—interview with Charlie Rose, World Economic
Forum, January 23, 2015

Relationship with the Government

When asked about interference from the government: I've never gotten one cent from the government. I've never gotten one cent from Chinese banks. So I am very independent. I had a very strict talk with my team: Never, ever do business with the government. Love them. Don't marry them. So we never do projects for the government. If they come to us and say, "Jack, can you help us with this?" [I say] good—I will introduce friends to you who are interested in doing that. Or, if you want me to do it, I do it free for you, just next time, don't come to me again. Because of that, we keep a very good love-relationship with the government.

—*60 Minutes*, September 28, 2014

User Experience

I use my computer and the Internet for two things: email and web browsing. Everything else is pretty much beyond me, even watching movies online. I ask our engineers for technology that serves people's needs. No matter how good that technology is, if people can't use it, it's worthless! Why is our website so popular with common business people? It's because I was the quality control—any programs written by our engineers had to be used by me. If I couldn't use it, it was trashed, because it meant that 80 percent of people as simple as I am wouldn't be able to use it either. My goal is that people can use it without even reading the manual.

—*Fortune Life Program*,
March 29, 2003

· ·

Change

Recently our personnel changes have been fre-
quent. I'm touched by the lack of complaint following all these changes. Things move fast in
these times and in our current culture of information exchange. Alibaba's staff needs to welcome,
embrace, and be ready for the challenge of all
these changes.

—Alibaba's 5th anniversary celebration,
September 10, 2004

· ·

Company Culture

Alibaba stands out not because our profits are
bigger or our staff is more talented. It is because
we emphasize foresight, strategy, system building, team training, and company culture from the
beginning.

—Qingdao Network Operators Meeting, July 22, 2005

••

Vision of the Future

We want to make the company last for 102 years. And people are curious: Why 102 years? Because Alibaba was born in 1999—last year we had one year, this century we have 100 years, next century, one year. With 102, we'll cross three centuries.

—Economic Club of New York, June 9, 2015

••

Acquiring China Yahoo!

He [Jerry Yang] said, "Call me." He said, "Jack, can you come and tonight we have our drink? For a final effort." And then I said, "Ok." So he took me to small, tiny Japanese restaurant and bought me big glass of sake. And we drank and [he] tried to convince me how wonderful Yahoo! is. And after drinking we said, "Ok, let's keep on talking." [That was] the most expensive sake I've ever had in my life. Now, I'm pretty sensitive about sake.

—interview with Jerry Yang, Stanford Graduate School of Business, September 24, 2015

● ●

Singles (Double Eleven) Day

It is not purely an online sales day. It is a day that the manufacturer, the business guys, communicate with the consumers. Consumers, it's the way they know the innovation, the new products, the new trends every year. . . . I think the American people, if they know that there will be products not only from China but also products from the Philippines, Kenya and Africa, Argentina, and all these nations, it will be unique.

—*Squawk on the Street*, November 11, 2014

This is a unique day. We want all the manufacturers, all the shop owners, to be thankful for the consumers. We want the consumers to have a wonderful day. It's special. Number wise, maybe there's not a big difference [in sales]. But for the event itself, the meaning of it, it's getting such great excitement in China.

—*Bloomberg Markets*, November 11, 2015

....

Alibaba College

Clients must be willing to undergo training after they become Alibaba customers. We will establish an Ali College early next year to train employees and clients. We want our clients to grow together with Alibaba. They can come to our company for training every month, or we can go to different cities and gather clients together for training. Our courses include Alibaba product usage, management practices, small- and medium-enterprise development, etc. This is what we run at Alibaba College.

—Harvard–Tsinghua Senior Executive Program,
December 2003

....

Taobao

The speed with which our Taobao website took off surprised the US media completely—they thought eBay was invincible! They weren't willing to believe a pure Chinese website could compete with major players such as eBay, Yahoo!, and others. But Taobao's user data forced US analysts to look at us with new eyes. Only then did they realize that C2C competition within China was far fiercer than anything they had imagined.

—*Reuters*, September 27, 2004

• •

Alipay

While Alipay now seems very successful, we were forced to come up with the idea for it. Back then, transactions on Taobao were difficult because we hadn't solved the problem of secure payment. Our big domestic banks didn't want to get involved, so we turned to foreign ones such as Citigroup and HSBC.

At a meeting that year, one executive advised, "How do you innovate and make decisions for your future? That's your mission." That's when we came up with Alipay. We do it cleanly and transparently, reporting to the relevant departments every quarter.

—*Zheshang Online*, March 31, 2011

• •

Investing in Health

China today, because of the pollution—of the air, of the food, of the water—we're going to have a lot of health problems. We can use our technology, our know-how to solve the problem. That's why we have to invest money today—to get ready for 10 years from now, when China has problems.

—*Bloomberg Markets*, November 11, 2015

• •

Investing in Happiness

Look at the world today. Especially China. The rich people aren't happy. The poor people aren't happy. The government officers are not happy. . . . I want people in China to enjoy the happiness of digital products—the movies, the theaters, the TV programs—all the digital content that makes the young people enjoy their lives, to be optimistic about the future.

—*Bloomberg Markets*, November 11, 2015

LEADERSHIP

....

Building a Management Team

Control of a company should never be about the number of shares a CEO holds. Rather, it should be about his or her wisdom and vision. Build your organization with a scientific, rational management team and don't allow any single investor or person full control.

—*Fortune Life Program*,
March 29, 2003

....

Laughter

When you run a business, you need to be able to laugh, too. A strong vision and active mind allows for this. Take pride in what you do, and be capable and strong. To be able to laugh and be proud requires sharp eyes and a broad mind.

—Ningbo Network Operators Meeting, June 11, 2002

....

Appreciating Employees

Hanging in my office as a reminder every day is a quote from martial arts novelist Jin Yong: "Great leaders know to treasure the talents around them."

—*Jiefang Daily*, September 4, 2008

....

Organizational Charts

In our company, the organization chart is reversed. The client is on top, employees are right below them, then the managers, the vice presidents, and me, the CEO, at the bottom. My bosses are the vice presidents above me. The vice presidents' bosses are the managers above them—and so on up with employees having clients as their bosses. As CEO, I am the "goalkeeper" on this soccer team. If the goalkeeper sees the most action on the team, that means big trouble, no matter the skill level.

—Shenzhen Network Operators Meeting, March 5, 2008

Team Spirit

Chinese businesses must pay great attention to team spirit. Cooperation comes from teamwork. Cast yourself as the singular hero above everyone else and suffer the consequences.

—Ningbo Network Operators Meeting, June 11, 2002

Being a Leader

Conduct yourself as a leader by being farsighted, broadminded, and capable and by working together with others. This is how I understand what it means to be a talented leader.

—Lakeside Academy, March 28, 2008

....

NBA Players

A good leader grooms subordinates who can surpass them. It is all right to have them struggle in the process. If you can't find a suitable replacement within six months, then you have problems in recruiting good talent.

A leader should look for the best things inside each person. They should be able to find strengths in each that the person may be unaware of. Seeing and nurturing this potential is critical to your power as a leader. What made me think of this? Watching NBA games.

These basketball players get better because all 12 players on each team want to be on the court. All of them think they are good enough to play, and this produces a lot of peer pressure. If you have such a system in your company, where there are no guarantees but judgment is based on performance, you will field a good team.

—Ningbo Network Operators Meeting, June 11, 2002

Vision, Heart, and Strength

The art of being a leader is nothing but three things: vision, heart, and strength. Vision allows you to learn more by traveling a thousand miles than by reading a thousand books. Learning as you go from what you observe will enable you to see farther than others. Inside your town, you might already be the most powerful. Then you go to Shanghai and encounter others further along than you. Go on to Tokyo and New York and the number of powerful people seems endless. Therefore, as your vision broadens, others will come to admire you. A leader must also have heart. Nine out of ten very talented people are eccentric. Their unique temperament already has them thinking that they are the best at what they do. Tolerate them. Your heart needs to be expanded and will be if you are self-disciplined in this way every day. Some people are very funny, sitting and sulking over trifles. They make themselves miserable because they lack heart.

—*Fortune Life Program,*
March 29, 2003

•••

Confronting Crisis

Of course Alibaba has faced its share of crises!
How else could I possibly remain this thin and
not gain even one kilo these past five years? I
once thought when your company starts to grow
the boss can relax a little. Instead, I'm more tired
than ever! An entrepreneur constantly confronts
crises—a good thing. Better to deal daily with
small pains inside the company before they turn
into a cancer.

—Hangzhou Network Operators Meeting,
September 15, 2007

•••

Soldiers Should Not Have Binoculars

In battle, soldiers should not have binoculars.
Otherwise, when the commander orders an as-
sault, the soldiers might think, "Oh crap, we can
see they have three machine guns, maybe we
should retreat."

—*Jack Ma's Quotations on Entrepreneurship*, 2008

. . . .

Loneliness

The day you become a leader, you will be very lonely. Even the second- and third-in-command will find it difficult to understand you well.

When the captain sets sail, sometimes he personally climbs up the ship's pole to see which way the wind is blowing. For myself, I need to think of things a year ahead of time, to consider the right systems and deployment of human resources to come. Success may be another year off, so decisions now may not be clear until then. But I can't enjoy success unless I'm willing to shoulder the responsibility of failure.

—Shenzhen Network Operators Meeting,
March 5, 2008

. . . .

Decisions and Mistakes

You act as a CEO only under two circumstances, neither during "normal" times. First, when you make a decision, and second, when you make mistakes. Always admit your mistakes and never look to find fault with your employees' execution or to blame your subordinates. A CEO shouldn't be preoccupied with claiming "success."

—Shenzhen Network Operators Meeting,
March 5, 2008

....

A CEO's Education

As a leader, a CEO's education must include getting out to see the world and thinking about what
he observes. . . . This is the way to bring opportunity and fortune to clients.

—Hangzhou Network Operators Meeting,
September 15, 2007

....

Nurturing Employees

Another function of a leader is to discover the
unique skills in every member of his team. In
this world, there are no bad employees, only bad
leaders and bad systems. Nurture carefully every
worker's potential without exhausting it. . . . In the
eyes of a leader, all employees are good. In the eyes
of a professional manager, all are bad. A leader
finds and utilizes the potential in all employees.

—Shanghai Network Operators Meeting, July 2005

●●●

MBAs

Last year, I sent four colleagues back for their MBAs—one to Harvard and three to Wharton. I told them, "When you return and have forgotten all that the MBA program taught you, then you'll have graduated. However, if you're still caught up in all the rules and regulations, you'll need to continue your studies. After two years pursuing an MBA, you need at least half a year to forget what you learned. That's real success."

—World Economic Forum's China Business Summit,
April 19, 2002

SUCCESS AND FAILURE

• •

Lessons Learned from Dark Days

The lessons I learned from the dark days at Alibaba are that you've got to make your team have value, innovation, and vision. Also, if you don't give up, you still have a chance. And, when you are small, you have to be very focused and rely on your brain, not your strength.

—Inc., January 1, 2008

• •

CEOs Make Mistakes

There is no CEO who does not make mistakes. Every successful person has faced frustration and made mistakes.

—Qingdao Network Operators Meeting, July 22, 2005

••

Learning From Experience

Actually, it's very easy to create a business. It's like walking in the dark, looking for light somewhere to guide you along. Only after 10 years am I comfortable now to talk about strategy and tactics. I prefer studying the reasons why businesses fail rather than why they succeed. People say that Jack Ma's leadership is the reason for Alibaba's survival. That's incorrect. I'm not that smart, but I am good at learning from experience.

—Guangzhou Network Operators Meeting,
March 21, 2005

••

The Four Qualities

Four qualities are needed along with talent: trustworthiness, team spirit, adaptability, and optimism.

—*First Financial Daily*,
November 24, 2005

Setting Realistic Goals

There is still a sizable gap between our top Chinese companies and large international firms. But while Western culture looks to big enterprise, here our 1.3 billion "ants" come from small- and medium-sized companies. This is where the victorious future lays, an army of Chinese network operators in small- to medium-sized firms besting big businesses. Be careful, then, in setting goals. If we set an unrealistic goal of a billion dollars in sales by tomorrow, we'll tire ourselves out in an atmosphere of failure. But if the goal is to run our company in a first-class manner without fixating on unrealistic numbers, we can have an army of 1.3 billion ants, clear-headed and ready to take on big elephants forever.

—Hangzhou Network Operators Meeting,
June 13, 2004

••

Employee Satisfaction

What's most important for a company's development in the 21st century? Employees. Treat them
with respect and morale is greatly enhanced. Employee satisfaction ties directly into a company's
prospects.

—Guangzhou Network Operators Meeting,
March 21, 2005

••

Handling Crisis

E-commerce can offer great contributions to the
future, but there will be a crisis now and then.
While it can be painful today and even more
painful tomorrow, it can be beautiful the day
after tomorrow. Keep on and hold on and always
be ready for the worst that may happen tomorrow. Then you'll get to see the sun rise the day
after tomorrow.

—press conference for Hong Kong Stock Exchange
IPO listing, November 6, 2007

● ●

Staying Positive

I am not the most talented person. My appear-
ance, abilities, and education are far from society's
best. But I understand human nature. You must
control the negative and build up the positive to
attain success. I try to do this through team spirit
and shared missions.

—dialogue with Kazuo Inamori, October 28, 2008

● ●

Working Hard

I don't know anything about computers so, as I
often say to the younger generation, "If Jack Ma
can succeed, then 80 percent of you can too by
working hard."

—*Fortune Life Program*,
March 29, 2003

● ●

Learning from Failure

If you only regret the fact you failed but not the
reasons for it, you'll always be in a state of regret.

—*Jack Ma's Quotations on Entrepreneurship*, 2008

....

Not Fearing Mistakes

Failure in a fast-moving Internet company, no matter whether you call it a brain freeze or a brain fever, comes from fear of making mistakes. Mistakes have to be made today in order to grow and run better tomorrow. Just don't keep making the same mistake!

—Alibaba's 2nd anniversary celebration,
September 10, 2001

....

Failure Begets Success

Strength accumulates from failure. If someday I brag to my grandchild all about my fine achievements, he or she may simply say, "What's so great about that? You simply rode the swelling Internet commerce tide in and found some investment." But if I talk about all my failures and mistakes in those years, then he or she may look at me with admiration. Final success includes many miserable experiences.

—Ningbo Network Operators Meeting, June 11, 2002

....

Jumping Too Soon

In 1999, Alibaba's early strategy was to skip over our domestic e-commerce market and immediately go international. We called this "jumping over a First Division Group A team to enter directly into the World Cup." However, from 1999 to 2001, Alibaba was not well known. Our focus was Europe and the United States, and I made many speeches over there then. My most miserable moment was at an event we organized in Germany in 2000. We set seats up for 1,500 people—only three showed up! I was very embarrassed but still had to go through with my speech.

—Qingdao Network Operators Meeting, July 22, 2005

....

In a Crisis Think of Clients

When disaster strikes, think of your clients. Then think of your employees and, after that, your competition. Actually, better not think about the competition because you need to handle your own troubles first. In dealing with a crisis, think of how it affects your clients and then your employees. If your employees are clear about how to react correctly, your survival for the long term is enhanced.

—*Win in China*, August 2007

COMPETITION

....

Embracing Competition

Competition is a must. It is a painful process that forces your company to grow. Choose the best to compete with, but never take it personally. Don't fight your rivals but embrace them and analyze their core concepts. No rival can kill you—only you can kill yourself.

—Shanghai Network Operators Meeting, July 2005

....

Enjoying Rivalry

Do I like competition? Yes. Competition allows you to improve yourself, be better, and in the process, make your rivals angry. An angry fighter is not a good fighter.

—Beijing Network Operators Meeting,
March 17, 2008

∙∙∙

Influence of Money

If everything could be won by money, then banks would control all the biggest companies. Running your business well against strong competition should provide a level of contentment that allows employees, shareholders, partners, and clients to all sleep well. In this way, the enterprise will become better and better.

—Beijing Network Operators Meeting,
March 17, 2008

∙∙∙

Crocodile in the Yangtze

Alibaba is like a crocodile in the Yangtze River. To fight with a shark in the sea is to lose. However, if we fight in the Yangtze River, we surely will not be defeated. eBay came to China to do battle in our native country where we have home-field advantage. Here it is ok for us to eat a bowl of noodles for ¥3 and rather stupid to spend ¥300 for the same. eBay invests ¥70 billion in the Chinese market to our mere ¥100 million. But what can they do better than us?

—interview with CNBC, October 23, 2004

• •

Stubbornness

Some will say they want to beat Taobao or defeat Alibaba. It sounds great, but really, only our own stubbornness can defeat us.

—Hangzhou 8th E-Businessmen's Convention,
September 10, 2011

• •

There Is No Winner

It's not about beating a competitor to "win," because there'll always be another competitor. Consider it more like an ecosystem of land, water, and biodiversity with all kinds of competing interests. This competition hones you and helps you to grow. . . . In such an ecosystem, the lion kills the antelope not because he hates antelope but because he needs to eat. You defeat your competitor not because of how powerful you are but because those who aren't willing to improve themselves remain stuck in the past and lose the future. If their technology is inferior, they must improve it. If their staff's quality is inferior, it must be made better. Think ecologically and look for a "win-win" with opponents. We're all in this together. Without lions, antelopes can't live to their fullest.

—Hangzhou 8th E-Businessmen's Convention,
September 10, 2011

....

eBay

It's unfortunate that Alibaba has no competitor. We get tired searching for competitors everywhere. Taobao, however, is lucky enough to have eBay as a great competitor. If you have to box with Mike Tyson, you might think yourself unlucky. But this type of world-class competitor is good. Think of your good fortune getting to play basketball against Michael Jordan. Taobao can learn a lot from a competitor such as eBay.

—*Beijing Morning Post*, October 21, 2004

....

Confronting Competition

When confronting competition, be mindful of four things. The first one is that which you can't see. The second is that which you look down on. Third is that which you can't understand, and finally, the fourth one, after trying all methods, is that which you can't follow up on.

—Qingdao Network Operators Meeting, July 22, 2005

* *

Pricing War

The question you must ask is: "If we fund a competitive price war with our own savings (not our investors' money) will we have full support?" The need in most companies is not so much capital and technology as it is critical thinking. Always ask who are you fighting for, why you are fighting, and how you'll fight. Then prepare for the worst. We must protect both the consumer's rights and the manufacturer's interests to the max. This is the key principle to success. If a price war for your "honor" uses investors' money to hold manufacturers hostage and deceive consumers, the cost is too high.

—internal speech to Alibaba employees,
August 27, 2012

* *

Identifying Competition

If you only have a small- to medium-sized Internet business, don't compete with NetEase, Sina, Sohu, and Alibaba on scale or size. Compete only on what you can do in the professional market that they can't.

—NetEase.com, February 17, 2004

• •

Ranking First or Second

We rank first in some of our industries and second in others. Some of our ventures fail to make money and die. Ranking second while still spending little, making good money, and being influential is fine. Indeed, some of our e-commerce is specifically targeted at this second position. However, none of our e-commerce is targeted for third place. Be either first or second, never third. If after two years of being third we cannot pass into second, then it is time to close that venture.

—speech to welcome China Yahoo! team to Alibaba,
September 23, 2005

• •

Strategy

If our competitor is loaded with bullets, we'll try to get him to shoot them into a wall. With the right strategy, competition should be an amusement, a game—not a source of pain. Conceiving the strategy of this game unites your employees and you. Remember, the first to lose their temper, loses the game.

—Shanghai Network Operators Meeting, July 2005

• •

Amazon

We are not competing with Amazon. . . . We have
a pretty different model. They buy and sell. Alibaba is a platform. . . . We believe every company
can be an Amazon. We think if Amazon is a great
apple, Alibaba is the apple tree. We want to enable
every company to be an e-commerce company.
We want a lot of people to be as successful as
Amazon.

—*Bloomberg Markets*, November 11, 2015

• •

Elephants

It's difficult for an elephant to step on all the ants
because the ants won't allow it. They'll run here
and there. And the elephant may break a leg trying
to step on them all.

—*Beijing Morning Post*, October 21, 2004

••

Copycats

Can Alibaba be copied? Our methods, maybe, but not our team and the wisdom gained from our mistakes. Nor can you copy my thoughts, our clients' trust, or the opportunities they've presented us. This does not mean that another company won't ever surpass us. We may see 100, 200, or even 1,000 e-commerce websites created. In the Chinese e-commerce market, I hope many more websites will innovate and exploit opportunities. If Alibaba's own site remains a work in progress, there'll be little need to copy us five years from now.

—Shenzhen Network Operators Meeting,
March 5, 2008

Your company's core competitiveness is your team and you. Others may copy your model, but not your constant persistence and passion. Behind the best innovation, of course, there must be a strong support system, talent, and execution. Without this, innovation is merely a story without value.

—*Win in China*, August 2007

MONEY, INVESTMENT, AND VALUE

....

Boards of Directors

Originally, Alibaba had a single board of directors to answer to our investors. Now we're divided into five companies, each one with its own board, to eliminate the risk of one investor controlling everything. While I respect shareholders and occasionally even listen to them, I act on my own ideas. I hear from my staff too, but still do what I think is right. But for customers, I'm all ears and try to follow their advice as much as possible. Customers first, employees second, shareholders third—this order doesn't change because of an IPO and the stock market.

—*Caijing Magazine*, August 1, 2007

• •

Investors

They love me, they hate me, but I love them.

—*Bloomberg Markets*, November 11, 2015

• •

Fiscal Responsibility

For successful business leaders, if their goal is to be rich, they can become very rich. But then what's the point of having all that money? When you have 100 million U.S. dollars, I think that's more than enough for you and your children. Once your net worth exceeds a certain point, that's not your money anymore. It is society's money. It is the money society has given to you, and you should take responsibility to allocate the money in a good way. I started thinking about this issue just two, three years ago. One day I suddenly woke up and wondered, "What's next?"

—Nature.org, December 2009

Saving Money

You Americans love to spend tomorrow's money. And other people's money, maybe. We Chinese love to save money. We are probably the largest safe deposit in the whole world. 'Cause we've been poor for so many years. When we made money, we put it in the banks, because someday we know that disaster is coming, and we can spend the money [then]. So when the economy is bad, we still have the money to spend. You guys probably don't.

—2015 Clinton Global Initiative Annual Meeting,
September 29, 2015

Weeding Out Speculators

In 1999, at a time when Internet companies were lucky to last eight months, we said our plan was to run our business for 80 years. This target of 80 years weeded out speculators interested only in chasing and cashing in on an IPO.

—Dongguan Network Operators Meeting,
March 2005

••

Shareholders, Investors, and Clients

In 1999, I told shareholders on the first day of financing that Alibaba's investors were our uncles. Clients are our parents. Since I get along so well with my "uncles," shareholders' meetings now run shorter than ever and are fun.

—China National Computer Congress,
October 12, 2010

••

Creating Value

If your CEO serves 10,000 clients, then your team should serve 100,000 clients. These 100,000 clients should serve 1 million clients. You create the most value when your clients can help other clients.

—Hangzhou Network Operators Meeting,
September 15, 2007

....

SoftBank

I know lots of smart people, but Masayoshi Son
[CEO of SoftBank] is unique. He may look dull
and speak weird English but he has great wisdom
even as he appears a little slow-witted. More than
700 companies apply annually for investment
from SoftBank. They invest in about 10 percent of
them, and Masayoshi Son negotiated directly only
with one: us. His words to me: "I invest in you because of your unique leadership. Keep it up!"

—preface to *Fly Higher*

....

Investment Is Like Marriage

Finding the right investment companies is like
choosing a marriage partner. We need to be hand
in hand through tough times. Today, everything
may be fine, but tomorrow, if our luck turns, I'll
need your support.

—Xiamen Network Operators Meeting,
September 2001

. . . .

Hong Kong IPO Listing

At a staff meeting in February I said we needed to prepare for when winter came. It was not a time to take things for granted. When speculation tripled our share price following our listing, I was mindful of dark clouds and thunder gathering even amidst the cheers and applause. Passion and fever that come quickly can fade with the same amazing speed. I wasn't willing to lose sight and lack reason concerning the sharp rise in share price.

During the listing ceremony, I said that we would go on as always. We would not change our mission. Forget share-price fluctuations and remember clients come first. We have a long-term promise to our clients, society, shareholders, and their families. When these promises are fulfilled, then our share price will naturally reflect the value created by the company.

—"The Winter Mission," email to Alibaba employees,
July 23, 2008

For the Alibaba Group, our IPO in Hong Kong today is only a beginning. We're fueling up in a gas station for a long trip ahead.

—press conference for Hong Kong Stock Exchange
IPO listing, November 6, 2007

....

Shareholding

Equity should be dispersed. Wisdom, not financing, should influence company management and employee teamwork. Our more than 1,000 employees are our biggest shareholder, with Masayoshi Son's SoftBank next. As market value grows, this management and employee shareholder ratio can be adjusted.

—NetEase.com, February 17, 2004

....

NYSE IPO

But when you have $1 billion, remember: That is not your money. That is the people's expectation of you. People put their hope on you, because people believe you can manage this money, resources, better than the others. If you think this is your money, you will be in trouble.

—interview with Jerry Yang, Stanford Graduate
School of Business, September 24, 2015

••

Making Clients Profitable

Why did we create Alibaba? Our goal is to make
our clients millionaires. We put clients first. Only
when they succeed can Alibaba then succeed. Our
profitability comes only after our clients become
millionaires and multimillionaires.

—Alibaba's 5th anniversary celebration,
September 10, 2004

Many of our employees wonder why they aren't
out in front, considering our "people first" policy.
We're not being hypocritical. When we gather
as a group to solve Alibaba members' problems,
we can't have distractions of "employees first" or
"shareholders first" taking focus away from resolv-
ing website issues. Whenever I meet with clients,
I want to hear that they make money with Alibaba. My biggest fear is hearing that they're not
profitable. So, when I meet with shareholders, I
can argue what our priorities must be even if they
don't feel good about it.

—Shenzhen Network Operators Meeting,
November 2005

. . . .

Financing

Never think about financing when creating a business. You will never create a good company that way. Don't chase after investors (they'll only run away faster) but know that, as a successful small-to medium-sized company, investors will come to you. Money will then be a happy surprise.

—NetEase.com, February 17, 2004

. . . .

Free Services

When we launched Taobao two years ago, we offered it free. Alibaba also provided three years of free service. Almost all of our services are launched free for the first year or two. The main reason is to understand our clients' needs during this period. Then we make adjustments accordingly. But if you find then that you can't generate any traffic even as a free service, it's hopeless. You may not have any value. We gained lots of valuable experience during our free period, so that today, things are very good. We now have USD$1 billion and can provide even more free service.

—*Fortune Life Program*, March 2003

Alibaba's Stock Price

I'm humble because I think many years ago people said, "Well, Alibaba's a terrible company." And I knew we were not that terrible. We were pretty good. We were better than people thought. But today, when people have a high expectation of us, I start to worry and become nervous, because we are not that good yet. We are a company that is only 15 years old. We are running an Internet business in China. The average age of the young people [here in China] is only 28 years old. So it's a young company, young industry, and it's not easy. When people have a high expectation of us, I want to tell myself and tell our team, "Be ourself. Do whatever we believe is right." I don't dare to watch the stock price . . . when people think you are good, you have to be sure that you're really that good. When people think you're bad, you have to be clear whether [or not] you are really that bad.

—*Squawk on the Street*, November 11, 2014

ENTREPRENEURSHIP AND INNOVATION

. . . .

Internal Email

We never promise that as Alibaba employees you'll enjoy nonstop promotions and share in lots of wealth. We do promise, however, that you'll have a steady share of our difficulties, depression, and pain.

If you've been with us less than a year, please spare us Alibaba strategy reports and development plans. Better you should open an exit door on your way out than your mouth. However, if you've been here at least three years, I'm all ears, happy to hear your suggestions for our growth, and grateful for your intention to make us better.

Remember, Alibaba doesn't pay you for your own personal development but for helping our customers in their growth. We develop ourselves through our customers.

—internal email to employees, August 27, 2011

What's Our Strategy?

One word: survival. Small and medium enterprises need unique survival methods. Opportunity exists in danger. A big crisis may take down larger companies, allowing small- to medium-sized businesses to emerge. Think through three questions: 1) What do you want to do? 2) What should you do? 3) How long do you do it for?

What do you want to do? You must have an ideal and a dream you're willing to give up your house for. What should you do? It's critical that you think about this from the very beginning. Easy to say, difficult to do. How long do you do it for? No matter the industry, count on at least 30 chances in your first five years. Insist on this principle no matter outside temptations and pressure.

—Beijing Network Operators Meeting,
March 17, 2008

Have a Dream

No matter what, you must have a dream. This is the best working capital to start with. Second, keep at it. There may be smarter people and more industrious people, but why did we succeed and make money when others didn't? We kept at it. Others didn't see a future for the Internet or the value in search engines, e-commerce, or a B2B network. While others went bankrupt, we kept at it. . . . Not thinking they'd find another job anyway, our employees stayed on and muddled through until we all became much better.

—Hangzhou Network Operators Meeting,
September 15, 2007

Domestic Consumption

My grandmother has only one shirt in her wardrobe. My mother has three; my daughter's generation, fifty. And 48 percent of them, eh, she never wears them. This is called domestic consumption. And we have to build up this kind of behavior and make people start to spend money. And this is something the government is not good at. We [entrepreneurs] know how to make this thing happen.

—interview with Jerry Yang, Stanford Graduate
School of Business, September 24, 2015

....

Money vs. Dreams

It's not about the money, it's about the dreams.
It's not only about the technology that will change
the world. It's about the dreams you believe that
change the world.

—Economic Club of New York, June 9, 2015

....

Gratitude

Understand who you are, the reasons for your
success. As to our present situation, we first need
to thank the emergence of the Internet. Without
the Internet, we could not possibly have such
revolutionary business ideas. Second, we need to
show gratitude for the high-speed development of
China's economy. For this, I thank my team. Having put up with me for five years, they still believe
in and follow me. But it's not Jack Ma who's very
capable and smart—it's my employees.

—Shenzhen Network Operators Meeting,
March 5, 2008

••

1,001 Mistakes

I call Alibaba "1,001 mistakes." We expanded too fast, and then in the dot-com bubble, we had to have layoffs. By 2002, we had only enough cash to survive for 18 months. We had a lot of free members using our site, and we didn't know how we'd make money. So we developed a product for China exporters to meet U.S. buyers online. This model saved us. By the end of 2002, we made $1 in profits. Each year we improved. Today, Alibaba is very profitable.

—*Inc.*, January 1, 2008

••

Start-Up Capital

In 1995, I started my business with nothing. Capital consisted of collective willpower and teamwork. Many entrepreneurs say without money they can't start anything. This is wrong. Entrepreneurs should be guided by responsibility and teamwork, not money. True entrepreneurs don't think of money first but only about their dream to start a company. Money is the final element.

—Alibaba's 5th E-Business Champions Grand Awards
Ceremony, August 2, 2008

• •

Company Size and Focus

Roughly speaking, smaller businesses rely on their operation, medium ones on their management, and big companies on their teamwork. For this team, there are three key things to have: a far-reaching vision, a broad mind, and an ability to accomplish big things. As Hu Xueyan once said, "The more difficult it is to start a business, the better the opportunity down the road as long as you can see that far ahead."

—Wenzhou Network Operators Meeting,
November 19, 2001

• •

Diversity and Innovation

A company's identity is somewhat similar to a zoo's. Just as a zoo is enhanced by having a wide variety of animals, so too does a company benefit from a talented staff representing all walks of life. This can only aid in innovation.

—"Lakeside Talk," June 24, 2007

Challenges

I never say that I'm a winner. Rather than claim success, I prefer to state that I conquer many difficulties. Every day, I face challenges and encounter problems that must be overcome. This is my main achievement. From day one, all entrepreneurs know that their day is about dealing with difficulty and failure rather than defined by "success."

My most difficult time hasn't come yet, but it surely will. Nearly a decade of entrepreneurial experience tells me these difficult times can't be evaded or shouldered by others—the entrepreneur must be able to face failure and never give up.

—interview on CCTV website, 2004

Bad Ideas

Bad ideas are OK. We're not afraid of bad ideas as much as having no ideas. Never be afraid of taking quick action to solve current and future problems. We review not only our own website but also that of other businesses and even our competitors to see what good ideas can be put into practice immediately.

—ICBU Mobilization Meeting, June 13, 2007

. . . .

Advice to Network Operators

Be ready for the difficulty and the daily grind. Nobody succeeds right from the start. I made lots of mistakes and gained lots of experience early on. For an entrepreneur, this is good. Don't just think about how much money you can make. If you do, you'll set yourself up for some painful lessons, especially for Internet start-ups. Today there may be many successful network operators, but none made money at all in their first three years.

—Hangzhou Network Operators Meeting,
June 13, 2004

. . . .

Crazy Innovators

You must be ready to bear the pressure, criticism, and loneliness that come with being an innovator. At first we were called cheaters, then crazy, and now complete lunatics. No matter what other people say, however, we believe in our company and ourselves. I don't care how others look at us but rather how we look at the world. Knowing how to move forward to meet your dream is the way of the entrepreneur.

—CCTV Innovation Forum, Beijing University,
December 8, 2005

● ●

Hashing It Out

As an extreme example, I would often disagree with what 90 percent of my staff agreed on at a company meeting. I think the best situation is when half of you agree and half disagree and you hash it out. Your competitors are also discussing these things, so it's a good test in finding your own way.

—Qingdao Network Operators Meeting, July 22, 2005

● ●

Small and Medium Enterprises

No matter what country, small and medium enterprises are the main source of innovation.
Once your enterprise becomes big, innovation concerns itself with the scale of the operation. At this point, my thought is that you always need to look outside your company for further innovation.

—Boao Forum for Asia, April 14, 2008

● ●

Young People

Well, trust the young people, trust this generation's innovation. They're making things, changing
innovation every day. And all the consumers are
the same. They want new things. They want cheap
things. They want good things. They want unique
things. If we can create these kinds of things for
consumers, they will come.

—*Squawk on the Street*, November 11, 2014

MEDIA AND MARKETING

∙∙

Naming Your Company

"Alibaba" is easy to pronounce in almost all the languages of the world. This makes it easy for all potential customers to accept and use our website name.

—interview with Charlie Rose, World Economic
Forum, January 23, 2015

∙∙

Advertising

Advertising can help in recognition, but branding is built by public response. It's a cultural value that can never be hammered home by advertising alone. Advertising increases costs and can reach a point where your client can't afford it. You must sustain a quality team and company culture, otherwise advertising will only bring added costs, not benefits.

—Alibaba blog, March 19, 2012

....

Expand Your Wealth Campaign

Communication problems can exist despite your best planning. In May, we held an important introductory "Expand Your Wealth" event at no charge. Everyone then expected future events would be free, too, but we found it necessary to have an entry fee. Although our competitors routinely charged for the same thing, we were criticized for this. We had no one to blame but ourselves for not having better PR and getting word out. In a new product launch for clients, there are four indispensible steps: convince them logically, motivate them emotionally, tempt them monetarily, and be fair and just to them.

—remarks to Alibaba executives,

June 16, 2006

••

Putting Words in Bill Gates's Mouth

In 1995, I explained incessantly that the Internet existed, but not many people were willing to trust it. They couldn't see how this Internet could be a great contribution to the lives of people.

I felt then that the Internet would impact all aspects of human life. But when Jack Ma said this, nobody would believe it. So instead, I started to say that Bill Gates was claiming the Internet would change the way people live. The media picked up on this. But actually, it is what I was saying then. In 1995, even Bill Gates wasn't a believer in the Internet. Later, I apologized to Bill Gates for this a number of times when I met him.

—Henen Youth Entrepreneurship Forum,
October 25, 2008

Being Jack Ma

Six years ago, our PR guy told me I had to start doing interviews. I resisted, unwilling to meet with any media. I feel I'm ugly enough that people remember me from first sight. If I walk down the street, everyone will know me. I didn't want this. However, after hounding me for three days, our PR guy said, "Jack Ma. This name doesn't just belong to you, it belongs to Alibaba." After that, I started to do interviews. From then until now, the media links Alibaba completely with Jack Ma. But please don't trust the media too much: The person they build up with praise one day can be brought down with attacks the next. Being "ordinary" is a glamour all its own.

—Qingdao Network Operators Meeting, July 22, 2005

••

Telling the Truth

Alibaba has a very good PR team, very capable. Our only secret is to always tell the truth. No matter wherever or whenever, say what you're thinking. Don't say things that the media loves to hear or deceive them in order to cater to them. Tell a lie now, and you'll be forced to keep it going even as you forget parts of it. This will only cause lots of pain. People like honesty. Not many people, however, will tell the truth at any time. Do so and you'll differ from others.

—Chinabyte.com, July 2001

••

Branding and Trust

Our promotional budget this past year was zero even as our name has grown greatly. This "miraculous" rise in branding has even caught the attention of the Harvard Business School. But there's no miracle. From 1995 through 1999, we had five years of hardship, but now, Alibaba will do even better next year. We learn not only from our own mistakes but from those made by other Chinese Internet companies, too.

—TrustPass press conference, March 10, 2002

. . . .

First Western Media Experience

August 1999 was the first time we met with the media. Somehow, *Businessweek* in the US found out about Alibaba. At first, we refused their interview request. Later, we accepted via the Ministry of Foreign Affairs and the Foreign Affairs Office in Zhejiang Province. At the time, we didn't even have an office telephone or fax machine. We did have a US address, however, so that we wouldn't be thought of solely as a local Chinese company and regarded globally as a third-class enterprise. For the interview, when we took the reporter to the residential area where we were based, they regarded us with suspicion. When we opened the door, we had 20 to 30 people crammed inside the four-bedroom flat. The interviewer thought Alibaba, with our big reputation and thousands of members, should have already been a very big company. In the end, that article was never published.

—Ningbo Network Operators Meeting, June 11, 2002

Building Credibility

A local Hangzhou newspaper implied in print that our private-enterprise Internet company lacked any real standing. In order to prove differently, we introduced our company with English PR materials sent from the US by courier. We printed out pages from our US website in color to show we were an international Internet presence. This was a difficult start. Later we realized that rabbits naturally eat the grass by their own burrows first, and we should have made friends locally from the beginning.

All this helps in credibility. I'm lucky now in that even if I were to leave this company, I could still finance USD$30 million with one telephone call. That's credibility. I have a large number of entrepreneurial students, and their trust is based on my credibility. Of course, you must use this credibility well and do what you say. We've walked the walk by relying on this belief.

—CCTV Innovation Forum, Beijing University,
December 8, 2005

· ·

The Internet

For us, the Internet is a tool. Why is it so power-ful? I'm a big fan of martial arts fiction. No matter how great a person's swordplay, however, someone with a gun can still kill them because it's a more powerful weapon. Compared with word of mouth from your relatives and friends or publicity from magazines, newspapers, and conventional media, the Internet will certainly become more powerful. If you miss this opportunity, you'll be out of luck. Never look down upon new and emerging tools. Use this new tool well and your enterprise will be better. Use it poorly, or not at all, and you'll suffer.

—Wenzhou Network Operators Meeting,

November 19, 2001

THE INTERNET, E-COMMERCE, AND GLOBAL TRADING

Bringing the Internet to China

So one day, later in 1996, China was connected to the Internet. . . . I invited 10 media friends to my apartment. I wanted to tell them, "I'm not telling a lie, there is a network called Internet." We waited three hours and a half to download the first picture. And people said, "Is that thing going to work?" And I said, "Yeah, it'll work, but not today. In 10 years, it'll work." But at least it proved I was not telling a lie.

—Economic Club of New York, June 9, 2015

∙∙∙

China vs. US

E-commerce in the US is a dessert. It's complimentary to the main business. But in China, it becomes the main course.

—Economic Club of New York, June 9, 2015

∙∙∙

Advice for China

From the American point of view, Amazon probably is the only business model for e-commerce, but no, we are different. . . . We show great respect for eBay and Amazon, but I think the opportunity and the strategy for us is helping small business in America go to China, sell their products in China. . . . China has been focused on exporting for the past 20 years, and I think in the next 10 to 20 years China should be focusing on importing. China should learn to buy, China should spend the money, China should buy a lot of its things globally. And I think that American small business [selling] American-branded products should use the Internet and go to China.

—Economic Club of New York, June 9, 2015

Advice for US Businesses

First, when US and international enterprises enter China, their biggest problem is dealing with Chinese bureaucracy. But rather than preoccupy themselves with *guanxi*, they need to create value for the Chinese market. Success in America doesn't guarantee the same in China, and it is crucial for these companies to adapt Chinese characteristics.

Second, leadership plays a very important role. In China, these international companies' leaders must have foresight in their pioneering efforts here rather than managing simply to safeguard established US and European brands.

Third, the Chinese economy is an entrepreneurial economy. Everyone is full of vitality and everything is possible. It's like Silicon Valley in the late 90s, with entrepreneurial passion and prosperity everywhere.

—Forbes Global CEO Conference,
September 21, 2004

. . . .

Making Money

They say these are the three *s*'s for commercial success: be strong, scalable, and sustainable. However, I think these three points cannot be achieved in the current Internet business model. Only a stupid businessman tells others how he plans to make money in a complicated and competitive situation.

—89th Canton Fair, April 13–26, 2001

. . . .

Feedback That Counts

Invariably, mistakes are made when starting a business. The important comments come from your clients—if users find your service useful, then it is. If they say it's useless, no matter what you say about it, it is. In e-commerce, electronics are the tool, commerce the goal. Investors can talk your product up to the high heavens, but if users regard your product without value or utility, you'll be crashing to earth in no time. As I say to my staff, "Don't tell me how to make money. Just tell me how to provide value to our clients."

—Xiamen Network Operators Meeting,
September 2001

Trade

Trade is a freedom. Trade is a human right. Trade should not be used as a tool against other nations.

—in conversation with President Barack Obama,
APEC CEO Summit, November 2015

New Type of Middleman

Some management experts claim it's hard to survive as a middleman. Therefore, I'm often asked if we will expand into selling or move to manufacturing to ensure future development. When the phone was invented, people said the post office was done for. However, the post office lives on. It's very difficult for one industry to completely replace another. E-commerce won't displace middlemen, but will develop with a new type of middleman. There are no "bad" industries, only bad businesses. This new go-between will rely more and more on technology skills. They will understand the changes that are needed. As such, they will surely be needed in the future, even a hundred years from now.

—*First Financial Daily*,
January 26, 2006

••

Role of SMEs

E-commerce is hot now. Many companies want to join in this Internet bazaar but have nowhere to turn for a successful example. They are reluctant to continue without proof it can help them profit. So, when asked to show them a successful project, I point to Alibaba. By gathering a large group of "shrimps," small- to medium-sized enterprises, we can attract whales to come feed on them. Small and medium enterprises then become the solution for successful e-commerce.

—TrustPass press conference, March 10, 2002

••

Counterfeiters

It's not white and black. If you just say, "Take that down," it is unfair to that guy [the seller]. We have to also protect these guys, not only the branded businesses. You have to care about all the people, their rights.

—*Forbes*, November 4, 2015

Chinese B2B

Asians in business believe it is better to be the head of a dog than the tail of a lion. Everybody wants to be their own boss and the Internet favors individuality even further. That is, the Internet user is self-centered, a brick on the Great Wall marked "I was here." When the Internet was introduced, there was already an overload of information. My goal was to do one thing: provide an "essence" of needed information that small- and medium-sized Asian companies would use all the time. The American model, based on being a big company, could spend a million dollars on software, but not many Chinese companies can afford that or even use such software. Chinese B2B emphasizes face-to-face communication between business people.

—89th Canton Fair, April 13–26, 2001

· ·

Small Is Beautiful

In the coming decade, the Internet will make the long-awaited transition from a marketing channel into a virtual infrastructure that will allow smaller companies, which are really the major engines of innovation, to compete effectively with major corporations.

The ability to identify or create new business opportunities around the world will be limit-less. For example, a business that starts in China or India will have ability to compete with one in Indiana. More importantly, the Indiana business that has the right attitude and global outlook will not only be able to compete with India and China, but also with bigger American and European cor-porations.

—*New York Times*, "Small Is Beautiful,"
October 26, 2009

. . . .

Credibility

After lots of research, we found that the number
one thing for e-commerce is trust and credibility.
Business people are most concerned with this.
Last year, both our national and international
media stated that while many people visited the
Alibaba website, there was a lack of trust because
it was based in China with mostly Chinese business users. They claimed that European websites,
although small, were like an intimate Internet
exhibition hall. Our large website was more like an
Internet bazaar. Later, we found ways to establish
a more credible system and plan to expand on this.

—TrustPass press conference, March 10, 2002

. . . .

SMEs

When I come to the SMEs, I always feel excited.
Because when I join the SME conference I see
from your eyes the dreams, the passion, the hope.
When I join the Fortune 500 conference, I see the
numbers, I see the revenues, I see the KPIs, I see
the bloody competition.

—APEC SME Global Summit, 2009

ENVIRONMENTALISM AND PHILANTHROPY

....

China's Obligation

The Chinese people really care about environmental protection in China. That will be their greatest contribution to the world. For me, I have the luxury to think about doing more for Africa. But how many people are like Jack Ma? How many Chinese people have the resources, the opportunity to develop a bigger world view, and have the luxury to see the outside world? Obligation to the world is good, but I think the Chinese people will say they have an obligation to take more action to take care of their own environment. If you don't or can't care for yourself, I don't think you can care for others.

—Nature.org, December 2009

....

Donating Money

Instead of simply donating money, Taobao can contribute more by providing good career prospects for 10 million people. If these people have no opportunity or income, a stable society is simply an illusion.

—Jack Ma's Quotations on Entrepreneurship, 2008

Donating money is important but not necessarily charitable. Donating that of which you have the least is real charity.

—Jack Ma's Quotations on Entrepreneurship, 2008

....

Philanthropy

Spending money is more difficult than making money. Especially for philanthropy. When you have a good heart, you should also have good knowledge and good capability to spend the money, otherwise you are doing good thing with good heart with a terrible way.

—interview with Jerry Yang, Stanford Graduate School of Business, September 24, 2015

Charity

Charity should not be done for publicity—it should be done quietly and anonymously.

—*Jack Ma's Quotations on Entrepreneurship*, 2008

Environmentalism

What we want to build up is consciousness and awareness among people. We want people to take these issues seriously so that they think polluting is just as bad as committing a murder. Because, ultimately, it is. Business is important, but it is just as important to take action on these environmental issues as well.

I'm not an extremist. We're just taking a stand on what we believe is good for ourselves and our children. And I don't want people to do it merely because they are told it is a responsibility. I hate the word "responsibility." I am taking action because this is something I believe in. It is a way of thinking and a part of my philosophy.

—Nature.org, December 2009

Climate Change

It's too late to complain, "Whose fault?" Whether your fault or my fault, let's solve the problem together.

—interview with President Barack Obama, APEC
CEO Summit, November 18, 2015

LIFE LESSONS

••

Three Principles

Always keep in mind these three principles: what you want to do, what you should do, and for how long you should do it.

—Beijing Network Operators Meeting,
March 17, 2008

••

World War III

The third world war is going to happen, and this war is not between nations. In this war, we work together against the disease, the poverty, the climate change—and I believe this is our future. That human beings, that nations, should unite together.

—Economic Club of New York, June 9, 2015

....

Personal Development

Pay attention to your own development and keep learning constantly. Never blame God or others for your position in life. Blame yourself.

—Shanghai Network Operators Meeting, July 2005

....

China's Slowing Economy

If China [keeps its] 9 percent growth of the economy, there must be something wrong. You will never see the blue sky. You will never see the quality. China should pay attention to the quality of the economy. . . . I think [it's] just like a human grows. This body can never [keep growing]. [At a] certain time, the growth of the body will slow. [Instead, you] should grow your mind, grow your culture, grow your value, grow your wisdom. I think China is moving to that direction.

—interview with Charlie Rose, World Economic Forum, January 23, 2015

....

Envy

Never envy another big company. Your current company is the best as long as you share common goals, missions, and values.

—Shanghai Network Operators Meeting, July 2005

· ·

Faith in Personal Beliefs

Be firm in your beliefs. Hold on to them, study them, and do the right thing by them. These four key points guided Alibaba's early steps. Without this faith, you cannot walk. My firm belief was that the Internet would influence and change China, that China would develop e-commerce, and that e-commerce would help make its users rich.

—Hangzhou Network Operators Meeting,
September 15, 2007

· ·

Teaching

My first occupation was teaching. If I can't now share my more than 10 years of entrepreneurial management experience with others, it'll be a waste. The more there is to share, the more to value and be treasured.

—dialogue with Kazuo Inamori, October 28, 2008

As a teacher, you always believe in the future. You believe knowledge will change people's lives. You believe and you hope that your students are better than you are. Students are the best prize. Today I'm not a teacher, but I call CEO the "chief education officer" of my school.

—Asia Game Changer Award ceremony, 2014

· ·

Obstacles

The long distance needed to reach your goal isn't the problem. The problem is not knowing just how far that distance is.

—Ningbo Network Operators Meeting, June 11, 2002

· ·

Realizing Dreams

Confirm what should be done to realize your dream. Often this involves taking a step back and letting something go. And be ready to give back and share with others at crucial moments.

—Shenzhen Network Operators Meeting,
March 5, 2008

· ·

Heroes

What I like about Hollywood movies is the hero. In Chinese movies, we also have heroes, but all the heroes in Chinese movies die. In American movies all the heroes survive. So I ask people, if all the heroes die, who wants to be the heroes?

—*Bloomberg Markets*, November 11, 2015

● ●

Telling the Truth

Students like my style. I believe that young people here are the same as me and like to hear the truth. I am thoroughly frank and honest with them. While telling the truth can be the most difficult thing in the world, it can also be the easiest. And when you tell the truth, people listen. When I criticize certain people it's because I love them. If they deserve criticism and I say nothing, it's because I don't like them.

—*Fortune Life Program*,
March 29, 2003

● ●

Changing Ourselves

Many years ago, I wanted to change the world. Now I think if we want to change the world we must change ourselves. Changing ourselves is more important and easier than changing the world. Second, I want to improve the world. Changing the world—maybe that's Obama's job.

—interview with Charlie Rose, World Economic
Forum, January 23, 2015

Never Give Up Today

Five years ago, my colleagues and I wanted to create the world's greatest company. Many thought such talk was mad. But no matter what was said, my dream to create such a company didn't change.

In the Internet recession of 2001–02 we talked only about "surviving." Even if all the other Internet companies died, we had to survive. And we did so only by refusing to give up, by believing in our dream. This incessant effort and constant ability to learn from our mistakes led to success. While today is tough, tomorrow can be even tougher. However, the day after tomorrow may be beautiful. But too many will give up after tough times on the eve of tomorrow night. Therefore, never give up today!

—receiving Economic Person of the Year in China
Award, December 28, 2004

MILESTONES

1964

Jack Ma is born in Hangzhou, Zhejiang Province, China, to two traditional Chinese storytellers.

1985

Ma visits a friend in Australia, where he realizes that the world is much different than what he was taught in school.

1988

Ma graduates from the Hangzhou Teacher's Institute with a bachelor's degree in English.

1995

Ma visits Seattle, where his friend introduces him to the Internet.

Ma, his wife Zang Ying, and a friend raise ¥20,000 and launch China Yellow Pages, a web development company.

1998

Jack Ma and the other 17 founders prepare to create China's first online trading market.

1999

Alibaba Group launches its website, a B2B e-commerce platform, in March.

Alibaba Group absorbs a USD$5 million venture capital fund led by Goldman Sachs and other first-class fund companies in United States, Asia, and Europe.

2000

Alibaba Group raises USD$20 million from investors such as SoftBank, Goldman Sachs, and Fidelity.

Alibaba Group holds the first West Lake Summit, a forum for Internet-business leaders.

2001

Alibaba Group launches TrustPass in order to better serve their international sellers.

Registered users exceeds 1 million, making Alibaba Group the world's first e-commerce website with more than 1 million of members.

2002

Alibaba Group turns a profit for the first time.

2003

Alibaba Group invests ¥450 million to create and launch Taobao, a C2C e-commerce platform.

Alibaba Group introduces the communication software AliTalk, which allows buyers and sellers to communicate instantly online.

Alibaba Group creates Alipay, an independent, secure online payment service on Taobao's platform.

2004

Alibaba Group receives USD$82 million from investment institutions such as SoftBank, Fidelity Investment, DFJ, and Granite, becoming the biggest private equity investment in a Chinese Internet company.

Alibaba Group hosts the first Netreprenuer Summit.

Alibaba Group launches Aliwangwang, an instant messaging tool, on Taobao.

Alipay becomes a separate company.

Jack Ma is named on of CCTV's Top 10 Business Leaders of the Year.

2005

Yahoo! purchases a 40 percent stake in Alibaba Group, investing USD$1 billion.

Alibaba Group takes over control of China Yahoo!.

Alibaba Group is chosen as the best employer in the annual CCTV Employer of the Year survey.

Alibaba Group pays a daily tax of ¥1 million to the government, one of the highest in China. This is a point of pride for Jack Ma, as it demonstrates the size and growth of his company.

Businessweek names Jack Ma "Businessperson of the Year."

2006

Taobao battles eBay for e-commerce dominance in China and wins—eBay shuts down its site in China.

2007

Alibaba Group launches the Taobao University program for e-commerce users.

The Hangzhou People's Government, Chinese E-Commerce Association, and Alibaba Group jointly organize and hold the Second Network Operators Festival in Hangzhou.

Alibaba.com is successfully listed on the main board of the Stock Exchange of Hong Kong in November for HK$13.1 billion (USD$1.7 billion), making the company the second-largest global IPO for an Internet company.

Alibaba Group launches Alimama, an online marketing platform.

2008

Taobao holds its fifth anniversary celebration, and Ma announces an investment of ¥2 billion in the Taobao website.

Taoboa launches Taobao Mall (TMall.com), a business-to-consumer retail website.

Alibaba Group launches the Alibaba Group R&D Institute.

2009

Alibaba Group celebrates its 10th anniversary.

Jack Ma creates Singles Day.

Alipay surpasses 200 million users, which means that more than half of Chinese netizens use e-commerce.

General Atlantic, a global growth-equity firm, invests USD$75 million in Alibaba Group.

Alibaba Group launches Alibaba Cloud Computing (Ali-Cloud).

Alibaba.com buys HiChina, the country's biggest Internet service provider.

Ma is listed by *Time* in its list of the world's 100 most influential people.

Ma is named one of CCTV's Economic People of the Year: Business Leaders of the Decade.

2010

Alibaba.com is renamed 1688.com

Alibaba Group launches AliExpress, which facilitates Chinese exports.

Alibaba Group announces an executive committee to spearhead the "Big Taobao" strategy, an effort to aggregate Alibaba companies and subsidiaries. The members are the executives from Taobao, Alipay, Alibaba Cloud Computing, and China Yahoo!.

Alibaba Group announces that it will appropriate 0.3 percent of annual revenues to an environmental protection fund to promote awareness about the environment.

Alibaba Group purchases Vendio and Auctiva, e-commerce service providers for US small businesses.

Taobao launches its mobile app.

2011

Tmall.com becomes an independent company.

Alibaba announces a warehousing network system in China and invests heavily in the Chinese logistics industry.

The SEC files submitted by Yahoo! reveal that Ma transferred Alipay ownership under the Alibaba Group to a domestically funded company (Alibaba Zhejiang), which is held by Ma and Xie Shihuang, one of Alibaba's founders. The battle to control Alipay emerges.

Alipay is authorized by the People's Bank of China and obtains a third-party pay license. It was one of the first 27 companies approved for this license.

Alibaba Group, Yahoo!, and SoftBank officially sign an agreement regarding the transfer of Alipay equity. Alipay continues to provide services to the Alibaba Group and its relevant companies, but Alibaba will also receive reasonable economic returns given by Alipay Holding Company.

Jack Ma clearly expresses his intention to acquire Yahoo! shares.

Alibaba Group and Yahoo! jointly announce that both parties have signed the final agreement regarding the equity repurchase. Alibaba spends USD$7.1 billion to repurchase 20 percent equity from Yahoo!.

Alibaba Network Co., Ltd. is officially unlisted from the Hong Kong Stock Exchange.

2012

Alibaba Group creates the Alibaba Foundation, which funds social causes.

Alibaba Group completes the preliminary equity repurchase from Yahoo! and restructures their relationship.

The Taobao website and TMall platform break ¥1 trillion in turnover.

2013

Taobao celebrates its 10th anniversary.

Jack Ma announces to employees that he is stepping down as CEO of the Alibaba Group.

Jonathan Lu becomes Alibaba's CEO and Ma stays on as executive chairman.

Alibaba Group launches Alibaba Smart TV OS and Laiwang, a social networking app.

In November, Ma is awarded an honorary doctoral degree from the Hong Kong University of Science and Technology.

Alibaba Group partners with private corporations such as Yintai Group, Shunfeng Group, Zhongtong, Yuantong, Shentong, and Yunda, to establish Rookie Internet Technology Co., Ltd. and starts the project construction of the Chinese Wisdom Backbone Network (CSN). Ma is named chairman.

Alibaba Group becomes a shareholder of ShopRunner, an American e-commerce, logistics, and distribution service that is owned by eBay. Alibaba takes the lead in second-round financing of ShopRunner, purchasing 30 percent of shares.

Singles Day brings in 170 million Alipay transactions for a total of ¥35 billion in revenue, an increase of 83 percent compared to the previous year's ¥19.1 billion.

Forbes ranks Jack Ma 30th on its World's Most Powerful People list.

2014

Jack Ma and Joe Tsai, a cofounder of Alibaba Group, announce the Personal Public Welfare Trust Fund. This fund comes from their options in Alibaba and represents about 2 percent of the Alibaba Group's total shares.

Alibaba Group acquires a 60 percent stake in ChinaVision, a film and television production company.

Alibaba (BABA) begins trading on the New York Stock Exchange at USD$68 a share. At USD$21.8 billion, it is the biggest IPO in history.

The Alibaba Group's market value reaches USD$238.332 billion, and Ma's net worth reaches USD$ 21.212 billion, making him one of the richest people in the world.

Time includes Jack Ma on its annual list of most influential people.

Alibaba Group purchases a significant stake in Youku Tudou, which is similar to YouTube but operates in China.

Alibaba Group launches Ali Health, an e-commerce platform that specializes in pharmaceuticals, health products, and medical services.

Alibaba Group purchases a 50 percent stake in the Guangzhou Evergrande Football Club for USD$192 billion.

Ma receives the Asia Society's Asia Game Changer of the Year Award.

2015

Forbes names Ma the 22nd most powerful man in the world.

Singles Day (November 11) generates USD$14.32 billion for Alibaba, a 60 percent increase from the previous year.

Alibaba enters India's e-commerce space by acquiring a 25 percent stake in Paytm owner One97 Communications.

Alibaba acquires the *South China Morning Post* and its assets for USD$266 million.

CITATIONS

Personal

Technological Ability

Jack Ma, acceptance speech for the Asia Society's Asia
Game Changer of the Year Award, United Nations, New
York City, NY, October 16, 2014, http://asiasociety.org
/video/jack-ma-small-beautiful-small-powerful

Achieving Balance

Jack Ma, interview by Charlie Rose, World Economic
Forum, Davos, Switzerland, January 23, 2015,
https://www.youtube.com/watch?v=aqSkQye85OQ

Learning English

Jack Ma, acceptance speech for the Asia Society's Asia
Game Changer of the Year Award, United Nations, New
York City, NY, October 16, 2014, http://asiasociety.org
/video/jack-ma-small-beautiful-small-powerful

Not Stupid

Wenjian Xiao, *Jack Ma's Quotations on Entrepreneurship*
(Beijing: China Zhigong Publishing House, 2008), 157.

Blind Tiger

Jack Ma, acceptance speech for the Asia Society's Asia
Game Changer of the Year Award, United Nations, New
York City, NY, October 16, 2014, http://asiasociety.org
/video/jack-ma-small-beautiful-small-powerful

Business Principles

Common Values

Jack Ma, "Alibaba's Development Strategy," speech
    at Network Operators Meeting, Ningbo, China,
    June 11, 2002, http://blog.sina.com.cn/s/blog
    _62ee908501000awo.html

Yuetian Han, "Jack Ma's Management," Xinhua News
    Agency, February 25, 2004, http://www.sinoec.net
    /article9956.html

Company Hierarchy

Jack Ma, speech at Alibaba's 10th anniversary celebration,
    Yellow Dragon Sports Center, Hangzhou, China,
    September 10, 2009, http://tech.163.com/09/0911/00
    /5IT0UL13000915BF.html

Building Strong Infrastructure

Jack Ma, speech at APEC Business Advisory Council's
    5th E-Business Champions Grand Awards Ceremony,
    Hangzhou, China, August 2, 2008, http://video.1688
    .com/video/view/122801.html

On Counterfeiting Allegations

Michael Schuman, "Why Alibaba's Massive Counterfeit
    Problem Will Never Be Solved," *Forbes*, November 4,
    2015, http://www.forbes.com/sites/michaelschuman
    /2015/11/04/alibaba-and-the-40000-thieves
    /#4264120c0b89

Motivation to Sell

Jack Ma, speech at Network Operators Meeting, Grand
    Regency Hotel, Qingdao, China, July 22, 2005.

Economic Recovery

Jack Ma, "Small is Beautiful," keynote address at APEC
SME Global Summit, Singapore, 2009,
https://www.youtube.com/watch?v=vG37c28L9B4

Key Performance Indicators (KPIs)

Cuodao Jin, "System, Culture and KPI" in *Jack Ma's
Management Diary* (Beijing: CITIC Publishing House,
2009).

Deception

Jack Ma, speech at Network Operators Meeting,
Shanghai, China, July 2005.

Succession Planning

Jack Ma, "How Can SMEs Survive the Subprime Crisis?"
speech at Network Operators Meeting, Great Wall
Sheraton Hotel, Beijing, China, March 17, 2008,
http://v.youku.com/v_show/id_cb00XMjI0MzMzMTY
=.html?spm=a26g8.7662898.0.0.iIryfS

Criticism

Jack Ma, speech at Digital China Forum, China Beijing
International High-Tech Industries Week, Beijing
International Conference Center, May 11, 2001.

Corporate Responsibility in the 21st Century

Jack Ma, speech at Alibaba's 10th anniversary celebration,
Yellow Dragon Sports Center, Hangzhou, China,
September 10, 2009, http://tech.163.com/09/0911/00
/5IT0UL13000915BF.html

Patience

Jack Ma, Q. & A. on ChinaByte.com, July 2001,
    http://news.xinhuanet.com/info/2013
    -07/15/c_132542748.htm

Perfectionism

"Know Yourself and Your Enemy, You Can Fight a
    Hundred Battles Without a Defeat," *Nikkei Business*,
    May 2002.

Wild Dogs and White Rabbits

Jack Ma, speech at Network Operators Meeting, Xiamen,
    China, September 2001, http://club.1688.com
    /article/5822103.html

On Hiring

Jack Ma, speech at Network Operators Meeting,
    Dongguan, China, March 2005, http://www.q00cc
    .com/dianshang/20141008/10717.html

Investing in Employees

"Know Yourself and Your Enemy, You Can Fight a
    Hundred Battles Without a Defeat," *Nikkei Business*,
    May 2002.

Alibaba and Other Ventures

Early Days

Jack Ma, speech at Economic Club of New York, New
    York City, June 9, 2015, https://www.youtube.com
    /watch?v=eh1c5G7gXQE

Smiling

Alibaba Group, ed., "Communicating with Alibaba's
    Cadres, June 16, 2006," in *Jack Ma's Internal Speeches*
    (Beijing: China Red Flag Press, December 2010), 154.

Business Model

Jack Ma, interview with Jerry Yang, 38th Annual
    ENCORE Award event, Stanford Graduate School of
    Business, Stanford, September 24, 2015, https://www
    .youtube.com/watch?v=kh_wPWQrWZA

Not Simply a Chinese Company

Fortune Life Program, first broadcast on March 29, 2003
    by Zhejiang TV, http://video.1688
    .com/video/view/92159.html

Thinking Differently

Jack Ma, speech at Network Operators Meeting,
    Dongguan, China, March 2005, http://www.qoocc
    .com/dianshang/20141008/10717.html

Focus

Jack Ma, speech at Alibaba's 10th anniversary celebration,
    Yellow Dragon Sports Center, Hangzhou, China,
    September 10, 2009, http://tech.163.com/09/0911/00
    /5IToUL13000915BF.html

Women in Business

Jack Ma, interview with Charlie Rose, World Economic
    Forum, Davos, Switzerland, January 23, 2015,
    https://www.youtube.com/watch?v=aqSkQye85OQ

Relationship with Government

Jack Ma, interview with Lara Logan, *60 Minutes*, CBS, September, 28, 2014, http://www.cbsnews.com/videos /jack-ma-brings-alibaba-to-america/

User Experience

Jack Ma, interview with Xiao Zhao, *Fortune Life Program*, first broadcast on March 29, 2003 by Zhejiang TV, http://video.1688.com/video/view/92159 .html

Change

Alibaba Group, ed., "Fifth Anniversary of Alibaba, Hangzhou, September 10, 2004," in *Jack Ma's Internal Speeches* (Beijing: China Red Flag Press, December 2010), 209.

Company Culture

Jack Ma, speech at Network Operators Meeting, Grand Regency Hotel, Qingdao, China, July 22, 2005.

Vision of the Future

Jack Ma, speech at Economic Club of New York, New York City, June 9, 2015, https://www.youtube.com /watch?v=eh1c5G7gXQE

Acquiring China Yahoo!

Jack Ma, interview with Jerry Yang, 38th Annual ENCORE Award event, Stanford Graduate School of Business, Stanford, September 24, 2015, https://www .youtube.com/watch?v=kh_wPWQrWZA

Singles (Double Eleven) Day

Jack Ma, interview with David Faber, *Squawk on the Street*, CNBC, November 11, 2014, http://www.cnbc .com/2014/11/11/cnbc-exclusive-cnbc-transcript -alibaba-founder-executive-chairman-jack-ma-sits -down-with-cnbcs-david-faber-today-on-squawk-on -the-street.html

Jack Ma, interview with Emily Chang, *Bloomberg Markets*, Bloomberg, November 11, 2015, http://www .bloomberg.com/news/videos/2015-11-11/alibaba-aims -for-50-revenue-outside-china-jack-ma

Alibaba College

Jack Ma, lecture for Harvard–Tsinghua Senior Executive Program, Tsinghua University, Beijing, China, December 17, 2003, http://www.oh100.com/a/201210 /180065.html

Taobao

Jack Ma, interview with *Reuters*, September 27, 2004, http://www.yesky.com/ColumnArea/217028202160193536 /20041027/1869222.shtml

Alipay

Pan Deng, "Jack Ma: Out of Necessity Comes Innovation," *Zheshang Online*, March 31, 2011, http://media.sj998.com/html/2011-03-30/283617.shtml

Investing in Health

Jack Ma, interview with Emily Chang, *Bloomberg Markets*, Bloomberg, November 11, 2015, http://www .bloomberg.com/news/videos/2015-11-11/alibaba-aims -for-50-revenue-outside-china-jack-ma

Investing in Happiness

Jack Ma, interview with Emily Chang, *Bloomberg Markets*, Bloomberg, November 11, 2015, http://www .bloomberg.com/news/videos/2015-11-11/alibaba-aims -for-50-revenue-outside-china-jack-ma

Leadership

Building a Management Team

Jack Ma, interview with Xiao Zhao, *Fortune Life Program*, first broadcast on March 29, 2003 by Zhejiang TV, http://video.1688.com/video/view/92159.html

Laughter

Jack Ma, "Alibaba's Development Strategy," speech at Network Operators Meeting, Ningbo, China, June 11, 2002, http://blog.sina.com.cn/s /blog_62ee908501000awo.html

Appreciating Employees

Jack Ma, interview with *Jiefang Daily*, September 4, 2008, http://finance.people.com.cn/BIG5/7789211.html

Organizational Charts

Jack Ma, speech at Network Operators Meeting, Shenzhen, China, March 5, 2008, http://tech.hexun .com.tw/2008-03-07/104268751.html

Team Spirit

Jack Ma, "Alibaba's Development Strategy," speech at Network Operators Meeting, Ningbo, China, June 11, 2002, http://blog.sina.com.cn/s /blog_62ee908501000awo.html

Being a Leader
Alibaba Group, ed., "Lakeside Academy, Hangzhou, China, March 28, 2008" in *Jack Ma's Internal Speeches* (Beijing: China Red Flag Press, December 2010), 9.

NBA Players
Jack Ma, "Alibaba's Development Strategy," speech at Network Operators Meeting, Ningbo, China, June 11, 2002, http://blog.sina.com.cn/s/blog_62ee908501000awo.html

Vision, Heart, and Strength
Jack Ma, interview with Xiao Zhao, *Fortune Life Program*, first broadcast on March 29, 2003 by Zhejiang TV, http://video.1688.com/video/view/92159.html

Confronting Crisis
Jack Ma, "The Rise of Network Businessmen," speech at Network Operators Meeting, Zhejiang Great Hall of the People, Hangzhou, China, September 15, 2007, http://tech.sina.com.cn/i/2007-09-15/10501741914.shtml

Soldiers Should Not Have Binoculars
Wenjian Xiao, *Jack Ma's Quotations on Entrepreneurship* (Beijing: China Zhigong Publishing House, 2008), 36.

Loneliness
Jack Ma, speech at Network Operators Meeting, Shenzhen, China, March 5, 2008, http://tech.hexun.com.tw/2008-03-07/104268751.html

Decisions and Mistakes

Jack Ma, speech at Network Operators Meeting, Shenzhen, China, March 5, 2008, http://tech.hexun .com.tw/2008-03-07/104268751.html

A CEO's Education

Jack Ma, "The Rise of Network Businessmen," speech at Network Operators Meeting, Zhejiang Great Hall of the People, Hangzhou, China, September 15, 2007, http://tech.sina.com.cn/i/2007-09-15/10501741914.shtml

Nurturing Employees

Jack Ma, speech at Network Operators Meeting, Shanghai, China, July 2005.

MBAs

Jack Ma, speech at World Economic Forum's China Business Summit, Grand Hyatt Beijing, Beijing, China, April 19, 2002, http://club.1688.com/article/8053314 .html

Success and Failure

Lessons Learned from Dark Days

Rebecca Fannin, "How I Did It: Jack Ma, Alibaba.com," *Inc.*, January 1, 2008, http://www.inc.com/magazine /20080101/how-i-did-it-jack-ma-alibaba.html

CEOs Make Mistakes

Jack Ma, speech at Network Operators Meeting, Grand Regency Hotel, Qingdao, China, July 22, 2005.

Learning from Experience

Jack Ma, speech at Network Operators Meeting, Guangzhou, China, March 21, 2005.

The Four Qualities

Xuepin Chen, "Yahoo China! Will Never Hunt Talents from Competitors," *First Financial Daily*, November 24, 2005, http://media.people.com.cn/ GB/40606/3888808.html

Setting Realistic Goals

Jack Ma, speech at Network Operators Meeting, Zhejiang World Trade Center, Hangzhou, China, June 13, 2004, http://blog.msn.soufun.com/5414606/143703 /articledetail.htm

Employee Satisfaction

Jack Ma, speech at Network Operators Meeting, Guangzhou, China, March 21, 2005.

Handling Crisis

Jack Ma, press conference for Hong Kong Stock Exchange IPO listing, November 6, 2007, http://tech.sina.com .cn/i/2007-11-06/18061836286.shtml

Staying Positive

Jack Ma, dialogue with Kazuo Inamori, Kyocera Headquarters, Kyoto, Japan, October 28, 2008, http://www.iceo.com.cn/zazhi/2008/1215/191174.shtml

Working Hard

Jack Ma, interview with Xiao Zhao, *Fortune Life Program*, first broadcast on March 29, 2003 by Zhejiang TV, http://video.1688.com/video/view/92159.html

Learning from Failure

Wenjian Xiao, *Jack Ma's Quotations on Entrepreneurship*
(Beijing: China Zhigong Publishing House, 2008), 138.

Not Fearing Mistakes

Jack Ma, speech at Alibaba's 2nd anniversary celebration,
Alibaba's offices, Hangzhou, China, September 10, 2001.

Failure Begets Success

Jack Ma, "Alibaba's Development Strategy," speech
at Network Operators Meeting, Ningbo,
China, June 11, 2002, http://blog.sina.com.cn/s
/blog_62ee908501000awo.html

Jumping Too Soon

Jack Ma, speech at Network Operators Meeting, Grand
Regency Hotel, Qingdao, China, July 22, 2005.

In a Crisis Think of Clients

Win in China, originally broadcast by CCTV-2 in August
2007, http://video.1688.com/video/view/114800
.html?spm=0.0.0.0.8cr8Lw

Competition

Embracing Competition

Jack Ma, speech at Network Operators Meeting,
Shanghai, China, July 2005.

Enjoying Rivalry

Jack Ma, "How Can SMEs Survive the Subprime Crisis?"
speech at Network Operators Meeting, Great Wall
Sheraton Hotel, Beijing, China, March 17, 2008,
http://v.youku.com/v_show/id_cb00XMjIoMzMzMTY
=.html?spm=a26g8.7662898.0.0.iIryfS

Influence of Money

Jack Ma, "How Can SMEs Survive the Subprime Crisis?"
speech at Network Operators Meeting, Great Wall
Sheraton Hotel, Beijing, China, March 17, 2008,
http://v.youku.com/v_show/id_cb00XMjI0MzMzMTY
=.html?spm=a26g8.7662898.0.0.iIryfS

Crocodile in the Yangtze

Jack Ma, special interview with CNBC in Alibaba's office,
Hangzhou, China, October 23, 2004

Stubbornness

Jack Ma, speech at 8th E-Businessmen's Convention,
Hangzhou, China, September 10, 2011, http://tech
.ifeng.com/internet/special/2011top10wangshang
/content-1/detail_2011_09/10/9100203_0.shtml

There Is No Winner

Jack Ma, speech at 8th E-Businessmen's Convention,
Hangzhou, China, September 10, 2011, http://tech
.ifeng.com/internet/special/2011top10wangshang
/content-1/detail_2011_09/10/9100203_0.shtml

eBay

Zhang Xuguang, "Jack Ma: eBay Has Lost the First Round,"
Beijing Morning Post, October 21, 2004, http://www
.yesky.com/ColumnArea/217028202160193536
/20041027/1869222.shtml,

Confronting Competition

Jack Ma, speech at Network Operators Meeting, Grand
Regency Hotel, Qingdao, China, July 22, 2005.

Pricing War

Sina Tech, "Internal Speech Reviewing the E-Commerce War with JD.com," August 27, 2012, http://tech.sina.com.cn/i/2012-08-27/11427550288.shtml

Identifying Competition

Netease Tech, "Jack Ma: The Story Behind the Investment," Tech Channel, February 17, 2004, http://tech.163.com/04/0228/15/0G856H7H000915B4.html

Ranking First or Second

Alibaba Group, ed., "Welcome China Yahoo! Team to Alibaba!" in *Jack Ma's Internal Speeches* (Beijing: China Red Flag Press, December 2010), 135–6.

Strategy

Jack Ma, speech at Network Operators Meeting, Shanghai, China, July 2005.

Amazon

Jack Ma, interview with Emily Chang, *Bloomberg Markets*, Bloomberg, November 11, 2015, http://www.bloomberg.com/news/videos/2015-11-11/alibaba-aims-for-50-revenue-outside-china-jack-ma

Elephants

Zhang Xuguang, "Jack Ma: eBay Has Lost the First Round," *Beijing Morning Post*, October 21, 2004, http://www.yesky.com/ColumnArea/217028202160193536/20041027/1869222.shtml